I0100378

Foreward

1 a world filled with distractions, finding meaningful moments of
nnection with our children can be challenging. Yet, the foundation of
hild's character is often built on the values and lessons they learn early
life. This beautifully illustrated book, "Letters of Love" presents 26
nildren's Devotions from A to Z as a bridge between adults and children,
fering an opportunity to explore some important scriptural themes
gether.

hy should you, as parents, grandparents, family members or educators
ad this book with the children in your lives? First and foremost, it
rovides a structured and engaging way to introduce young minds to daily
prayer practices that will help guide them throughout their lives. Each
letter of the alphabet represents a unique scripturally based devotion,
making it easy to incorporate these lessons into your daily routine. The
simplicity of the A to Z format helps children to grasp the devotional
content while allowing you to reinforce
these ideas through discussion and reflection.

Moreover, these devotions are designed to foster spiritual growth, scripture
memorization,
and a sense of purpose in their young hearts. By reading and reflecting on
these devotionals your child will learn to apply scripture to their lives and
journal their thoughts.

Letters of Love is more than just a book; it's an invitation to embark on
a discipling journey of faith, discovery, and connection with your child.
Whether you are looking to instill a sense of growing confidence, nurture a
budding spiritual curiosity, or simply spend quality time together seeking
the heart of the Father, this book is the perfect starting point.

- Reverend Clifton McDowell
  Pastor of the Church of God of East New York
  Presiding Elder - Eastern New York General Assembly

LETTERS OF LOVE :
26 DAILY DEVOTIONS FOR YOU CHILD

Written by
Nicole Patrice Thomas

Illustrated by
Elijah Tan

Copyright © 2024 by Nicole Patrice Thomas
All rights reserved. This book or any portion thereof may not
be reproduced or used in any manner whatsoever without the
express written permission of the publisher except for the use of
brief quotations in a book review.

Printed in the United States of America
Cover Design By Elija Tan
Illustrations By Elija Tan
NIV Scripture References
First Printing, 2024
ISBN 978-1-7372986-8-7

Introduction

This devotional is intended to help children memorize scripture in a way that will be both memorable and relatable. The scriptures in this devotional have been selected with prayer, and the breakdown written with love and care. I hope you and your child will read these pages and be blessed. May they inspire conversation and ultimately assist, as you lead your little ones closer to the Father.

To _____,
For this child we have prayed.

Above all else, Guard your heart. For Everything you do flows from it.
Proverbs 4:21

Have you ever eaten too much candy at a birthday party? Or gobbled so much cake you felt sick? What happened next? Yep, yuck, it all came up and out mighty quick!

Or have you tried to fill your cup to the very tippy top with your favorite juice, but then someone bumps into you, and *WHOOSH*, it spills over making a big mess?

In the same way that bad ideas bring bad results, good thoughts fill our hearts with good things. If we hold onto things that are not good for us, or we fill our hearts with angry feelings, jealousy, or bad words, eventually something will happen, and what's inside us will tumble out. Maybe someone steps on your toe or your sibling breaks your favorite toy, you might get angry and push them or say a bad word.

God wants us to store good things in our hearts, so when bad things happen, His love is what spills out.

Father, help me to keep good things in my heart, so when bad things happen your love will flow out. Amen.

Be strong and courageous. Don't be afraid, don't bediscouraged, for the Lord your God is with you wherever you go.
Joshua 1:9

Have you ever had to move to a new neighborhood, start at a new school, or join a new team? Were you afraid? Did you feel uncertain about what would happen? Maybe you were scared that you wouldn't make new friends.

God understands that we'll have those feelings sometimes. But he also wants us to know that even when we do feel that way we can be brave and strong. Why? Because He PROMISED to be with us wherever we go, and God never breaks a promise.

Next time you feel afraid or uncertain, say this prayer:

God, you promised to be with me wherever I go. I trust you because you never break your promises.
Help me to be brave. Amen.

Come to me, all you who are weary and burdened,
and I will give you rest.
Matthew 11:28

The year 2020 was really hard for a lot of people. We were stuck indoors for weeks. We couldn't see our friends or hug our nanas or papas. We missed birthday parties and vacations. And for some of us, we lost people we loved.

That's enough to make even the strongest person in the world miserable. That sadness sometimes feels like a burden on our shoulders or a weight on our chest. It can be hard to express with words the things we feel.

Just as you can talk to your parents when you're feeling down, God wants us to go to Him when we feel that way as well. He understands. Even if you're just sitting quietly and thinking about all the stuff going on inside you, your thoughts, your sighs, and even your tears are like a special language that God understands.

Go to Him and He will help carry those gloomy thoughts and feelings.

Father, I feel very _____ *right now. I don't have all the words to say it, but I know you understand and love me. Help me find peace. Amen.*

My Thoughts

My Thoughts

Do to others what you would have them do to you.
Matthew 7:13

Sounds like such an easy thing to do! But have you ever taken your sibling's favorite toy or the last slice of pizza even though you knew someone else wanted it? Maybe it's something like rushing to always be first in line and bumping someone who is slower than you out of the way. You wouldn't want someone to do that to you, right? It isn't a good feeling.

Next time you are tempted to take the best or the first or the biggest for yourself, think about the person next to you or behind you. Imagine how special they would feel if you saved the best for them!

It's not something that comes easily. Each day we must think about how our actions will make someone else feel. God wants all of us to have the best. It doesn't matter what color we are or where we are from. It doesn't matter if we're in a wheelchair or have full use of our bodies. No matter how different we are, God loves us equally and wants us to treat each other with that same love.

Father, please help me to put others first.
Let me love them and treat them as I would like to
be loved and treated. To see others, no matter how different
we are, as you see them. Amen.

Everyone who hears these words of mine and puts them into practice is like a wise man who built his house on the rock.
Matthew 7:26

Have you ever built a sand castle or a pillow fort? The most important part is the bottom, right? If you started your sandcastle too close to the water, the foundation would be soft and it would fall apart pretty quickly. If you tried to build your pillow fort on a water bed, it would swish all over the place every time you moved!
That would be funny, but it wouldn't last long.

I'm sure you've heard the story of the Three Little Pigs who tried to build their homes from three different materials. One used sticks, one tried straw and the clever one built with bricks. Which one stood up against the big bad wolf?

The same can be said for our lives. Scripture and the promises of God are our strong foundation, the bricks that build a wall of protection around us. If we stand on those scriptures and promises, they will keep us strong and secure! When bad swishy things try to make us unsteady, too bad! We won't be knocked down. When someone huffs and puffs and tries to blow our house down, we will be safe and warm inside.

Father, help me to use your words to build my life.
Help me to store them in my heart, so that they can become like brick walls that will keep me safe and secure. Amen.

For I know the plans I have for you, plans to prosper you and not to harm, plans to give you a hope and a future.
Jeremiah 29:11

God knows your name. He created you for a very special reason. From the moment your heart started beating in your mommy's belly, before she even knew you were there, God knew you and had a plan for your life. Maybe you're really good at drawing or painting. Maybe you love science and experiments, or you have a really great imagination for telling stories! Perhaps you're awesome at making others feel special or happy. These are all things God gave you to help you achieve those plans
He's made for your future.

Those plans are good, REALLY good, GREAT even! But because we're human, it's hard to know exactly what those plans are and waiting can be hard. But what do we say? God never breaks a promise! He said He has plans for your future, so you can trust in His word. Pray every day that He will show you what you were created for, and how you can use your natural gifts to find out His plans for your life.

Father, I know you made me for a very special reason. Thank you for thinking of me, and for making me good at _____. Please lead me every day, down the path you want me to go, so we can reach my purpose together! Amen.

My Thoughts

My Thoughts

Great is our Lord and mighty in power; his
understanding has no limit.
Psalms 147:5

Think of the strongest person you know. Maybe it's your dad or
your big brother. Maybe it's a gym teacher or coach. God is even
stronger than that! There is nothing too hard for God to do or
understand. There's nowhere that He can't go, and there's no one
He can't help. He created everything you see from the tiniest ant
to the tallest mountain and the shooting stars.

And He made you! That means you are pretty awesome too!

*Father, thank you for all the wonderful things you have
created. Thank you for understanding me. Amen.*

Honor thy father and mother.
Exodus 20:12

Other than God, there is no one on this whole earth who will love you as much as your mother and father do. They want the very best for you and will do everything possible to love, care, protect and guide you. That includes giving you rules and boundaries, and telling you what to do. They do this because they love you and don't want anything bad to happen to you.

They want you to develop good habits,
morals and to be responsible.

The best way that you can show you love and honor them is by being obedient. If they ask you to clean your room and you don't do it, or they tell you to finish your homework before watching your favorite show and you ignore them – that is not honoring them. If you're with friends and they're doing something you KNOW your parents have told you not to do but you do it anyway, that is not honoring them. It doesn't matter if your parents see your actions or not, because you know what to do you must choose to do the right thing to honor them.

God expects obedience. Through His word, the Bible, we are given rules and instructions to obey. They show us God's love and desire to protect us and provide the best for us.
Unlike our parents, He can ALWAYS see whatever we're doing, so be sure you are honoring Him in whatever you do.

Father, help me to honor you and my parents.
Help me to be obedient in every situation,
as I have been taught. Amen.

I am the vine, you are the branches.
John 15:5

What is your last name? Is it the same as your mom or dads?
That means you are part of the same family. Sometimes, families
don't have the same name, and that's OK.
The love you share makes you part of the same family.

Have you ever looked at a rose or flower bush? Or if you have a
vegetable garden, have you looked at a tomato plant? Did you
notice how there is one body and lots of smaller branches that
come off it? No? How about you go and investigate,
and then make a drawing of what you see.
Pay attention to all the different shapes and sizes.

You may not have the same name as other members of your
family, but the love you have for each other
makes you one family.

Just like that, you're also a member of God's family. He is the
main body and you are one of the many branches that come
from Him! Everyone who loves and obeys God is one of those
branches spreading out into the world.

Father, thank you for making me a part of your family.
Help me to stay connected to you always. Amen.

My Thoughts

My Thoughts

_____

_____

_____

_____

_____

_____

_____

_____

_____

_____

_____

_____

_____

Jesus Christ is the same yesterday, and today, and forever.
Hebrews 13:8

Do you have a best friend? Have you always been close? As we grow up, sometimes people change and we stop being friends. Maybe you both played the same sport or the same instrument in the beginning. But now one of you would rather play something different, so you don't spend as much time together. Or maybe you had a fight and don't even know why you were arguing, something just changed. Unfortunately, this happens. The only time it does NOT happen is with Jesus.

Jesus never changes. He won't decide to love you today but not tomorrow. His love, His power, His forgiveness, EVERYTHING about Him is eternal. What does that mean? It means His character never alters and His love never ends. Therefore, because He is constant and never changes, we can trust Him. We might change, but God never will.

He promised.

Father, thank you for never changing.
Thank you for being reliable and trustworthy. Amen.

Keep your tongue from evil and your lips from telling lies.
Psalms 34:13

When was the last time you told a lie? Today? Yesterday? Last week? Whenever it was, did you notice that you had to tell another lie to keep the first one covered? Lies are like snowballs on the top of a hill. Once it gets started, it gets bigger and bigger and bigger until it destroys everything it hits. It destroys trust and confidence. It destroys reputations and friendships. Nothing good will ever come from telling a lie.

Scripture tells us to keep our tongues from evil and from telling lies because God wants to protect us from the destruction those things cause. Is telling the truth easy? Not all the time. If you break your grandmother's favorite glass and she asks you about it, if you tell the truth you might get punished. But if you tell a lie and blame the cat or your little brother, not only will you make God sad, but when the truth comes out that you broke it and lied, you could get punished twice!

If you let telling lies become a habit, just like the boy who cried wolf, no one will believe you when you really need them to. Make it a habit to be honest, to tell the truth, and to live a life of integrity. You will be proud of yourself if you do, and so will God.

Father, help me to say and speak only those things that are good and truthful. Help me to be an honest person. Amen.

Let your light shine before men, that they may see your good deeds and praise your father in heaven.
Matthew 5:16

Have you ever helped someone because it was the right thing to do, and then later you were congratulated by someone, maybe your mom, dad or teacher? And you didn't even know they'd been watching you! That is because you've been taught by the people who love you to be a kind and caring person. They want you to do good things for others even when you think no one is looking.

Look into a mirror and tell me what you see. Maybe you have your mom's hair color or your dad's smile, you are a perfect blend of your parents, a reflection of their love.
God wants you to be a reflection of Him as well. So when people look at you and see the things you do, let them see His love shining through you.

Father, help me to be a reflection of your love for the whole world to see. Help me to shine brightly in the darkness and point others toward you. Amen.

My Thoughts

My Thoughts

Make a joyful noise unto the Lord
Psalms 98:4

What is your favorite season of the year? Mine is spring! It's not too hot or too cold and everything is being renewed. If you have allergies (like me), spring may not always be such a good thing! Achoo! Despite my hay fever, I love to see flowers bursting through the dirt and to take notice of their beautiful colors. I also love all the different shades of green that show trees waking up after a long sleep. And shush ... can you hear the birds singing? Sometimes I close my eyes and listen to the wind as it blows through the trees, or watch how the branches sway like arms waving in the air to music only God hears.

Every creature on earth has the potential to make a joyful noise and praise our Father. That includes me and you! We can sing. We can dance. We can clap our hands. Even something simple like yelling THANK YOU JESUS, or maybe whispering it softly if you're indoors, makes His heart glad. He loves to hear our praises in whatever form we release them.
So go ahead, make a joyful noise!

Father, thank you for all you have created!
I worship and praise you with joy.
Accept my praise. Amen.

N o man can serve two masters.
Matthew 6:24

Imagine you get home from school and on the counter are yummy freshly baked chocolate chip cookies! You ask your mom for one, but she says not until after dinner. She tells you to get started on your homework as she heads outside to work in her garden.

There you are, all alone with warm, gooey, chocolate chip cookies and a small voice whispering, *what if she doesn't see you take it?* What do you do? Do you obey your mother or listen to that voice inside your head? I hope you choose to be obedient because the alternative will get you into a lot of trouble.

We have a choice in everything we do. We can be obedient to our parents, teachers and God, or we can do whatever we want without thinking of the consequences. But we cannot do both. Obedience shows that we love and respect those who set the rules for our protection; disobedience says we only care about ourselves and our desires.

You have to be strong to resist temptation. You have to make the choice of which master you will serve. And maybe dad will slip you a cookie while you're doing your homework!

Father, help me to be obedient to you and to those in authority. Help me to be strong and wise in my decisions. Amen.

O give thanks to the Lord, for He is good; His love
endures forever.
Psalms 118:1

Do you say grace before you eat your food? Or say prayers at bedtime? I know sometimes we are so hungry or so tired that we forget, but it is important to thank God for everything. He loves us so much that He provides everything we need: food, clothing, shelter, family, friends, puppies, kittens, cookies, and ice cream too!

Nothing is too small or too silly to thank Him for.

So remember, God loves to hear from us. Next time you bow your head to give thanks, thank Him for His love too!

Dear Father, thank you for who you are and all that you do for us. Thank you for everything you have given us. Thank you for loving me. Amen.

My Thoughts

My Thoughts

Pleasant words are a honeycomb, sweet to the soul and healing to the bones.
Proverbs 16:24

I am sure you have heard the phrase, "Sticks and Stones can break my bones, but words will never hurt me", and I'm sure you also realize that it's not entirely true. Yes, objects can physically hurt us, but words can hurt us in places deep inside where no one but God can see. In the same way, kind words can heal those places that have been hurt.

While kind words cannot physically heal a broken bone or a wound, they can go a long way in making someone feel better. Have you ever had a really rotten day and then someone paid you a compliment? Did it make the day just a little bit better? Maybe it made you smile, and you realized things were not as bad as you thought. That is the power of pleasant and kind words! It's kind of like a superpower!

So go out there and be SUPER!
Make someone else's day better by saying something nice!

Dear Lord, help me to use my words to make someone feel better. Help me to say things that are good, kind and pleasing. Amen.

Quiet words of the wise are more to be heeded than theshouts of a ruler of fools.
Ecclesiastes 9:17

My dad doesn't yell. So when he does speak, we all know he has something important to say and we had better pay attention. People who always talk really loudly or need to yell over everyone else usually don't have anything important to say. They just like to be heard.

You want to be the kind of person that people listen to. When you speak, you want people to say _____ is talking, and they always have something good to say, so I better listen. Try your hardest to be wise, so you can help people make good decisions and find better ways to get things done.

Lord, help me to use my words wisely.
Help me be a person that others want to listen to. Amen.

Remember the days of old; consider the generations long past. Ask your father and he will tell you, your elders, and they will explain to you.
Deuteronomy 32:7

Do you know someone who thinks they know it all? Do you think you know it all? I have news for you then, no one knows it all except God (because He made it all, doh!). There are ways you can learn besides just going to school or reading or using the internet.

Ask people who are older than you to share their stories with you. Your dad, grandpa, mom or grandma, and maybe you could even ask your great-grandparents! How did the way they grew up differ from how you're growing up? Was it harder or easier? Did they want the same things you do now?
Ask how they learned about God.
What is the best thing God has ever done for them?
How does God show them that He cares for them?

You can learn so much about God's love for you,
by learning how God loves those around you!

So go ahead, ask away today!
And hey, why not ask God to pop the right questions into your mind?

My Thoughts

My Thoughts

_____

_____

_____

_____

_____

_____

_____

_____

_____

_____

_____

_____

_____

Seek first his kingdom and his righteousness,
and all these things will be given to you as well.
Matthew 6:33

Sometimes we want to skip to the good part of life. I know I feel like that often. But life doesn't work that way, does it? There are hard things we all have to go through and deal with in order to reach the good part that God has planned for us. (Remember, he has good things planned for our future because we love him!) To get to those good things that He wants to give us, we have to seek HIM first.

What does that mean?

It means we ask God for advice and instructions before making decisions, we SEEK His direction.
It means we repent when we do something wrong, we SEEK His forgiveness.
It means telling our friends and family about His love and goodness, we SEEK His kingdom.
It means doing what He tells us to, being obedient to His will, we SEEK His righteousness.

When we consistently try to do all those things with our whole heart, He will give us the good things He wants us to have. I say try because no one is perfect (except Jesus) so we will fail sometimes, but keep trying. God sees your effort and will be so pleased with you!

Lord, please help me to seek your direction, your forgiveness, your kingdom and your rightousness. Help me to see YOU with my whole heart ever day. Amen.

The fruit of the spirit is love, joy peace, patience, kindness, goodness, faithfulness, gentleness, & self-control.
Galatians 5:22

Actions speak louder than words. Have you heard that said before? That means that what you do, tells people more about you than what you say. If you say you love your pet but you don't feed it or clean up after it, your actions say you don't really love it. If your parents said they loved you but always forgot to pick you up from school or make you dinner, would you feel loved? Probably not. What is in you will always come out in your actions. Input, Output.

When you're kind, patient, gentle, show self-control and the other traits in the verse, you're showing that the Spirit of God lives in you! And did you notice they are all GOOD things? God only wants what is best for us. What are some ways you could show the fruits of the spirit in your daily life?
Can you write down a long list?

Dear Lord, please help me to better show your Spirit in my life. Help me to be good and kind to others, like you are good and kind to me. Amen.

Under his wings you will find refuge.
Psalms 91:4

If you have ever visited a farm, you may remember seeing chickens. Do you remember seeing baby chicks? If not, it could be because their mama was hiding them! A mama chicken will puff up and spread her feathers over the babies, so not one of them can be taken from her. Some will spread their wings wide and cover them from the rain!

Now, imagine Jesus doing that for you. He spread his arms so wide that He covered the whole world and everyone in it, even the people not born yet! He doesn't want to lose a single soul.

Do you know what refuge means? No? Well, answer this: When you're really afraid or hurt where is the one place you go? Do you run to mom or dad, or maybe your nana or papa? Wherever you go or whoever you run to first that is your safe place. Your REFUGE.

God wants to be a refuge for us too. When we're hurt or sad, He wants us to run to him first. Why? Because He is the SAFEST! He will never leave us, lie to us, or hurt us. Run to him! His arms are always open to you.

Father, thank you for protecting and shielding me.
Help me to remember that you are my refuge and safe place.
Remind me that I can run to you and you'll hide me
beneath your gentle wings. Amen.

My Thoughts

My Thoughts

V engeance is mine says the Lord.
Romans 12:9

When someone is mean to you, it's really hard not to turn around and be mean right back.

God is telling us not to be mean back at them. When someone is horrid – be extra nice to them instead. When someone hurts you – pray for them. When your sibling breaks your favorite toy or ruins your best dress or eats the last piece of cake – don't get even!

God will take care of it! Even though that is really, really hard to do, you have to trust God's promises. Leave it in his hands, because if you do something mean or hurtful to the other person, you will make God sad!

That's not what we want, right? Let God punish those who do wrong and reward those who do right.

I don't know about you, but I like rewards much better than punishments!

Dear Lord, help me to love those who hurt and treat me badly. Help me to trust that you will take care of me always. In Jesus' name, Amen.

W ait for the Lord; be strong and take heart
and wait for the Lord.
Psalms 56:3

I think waiting is one of the hardest things to do. That could be
why the Bible tells us to be strong while we wait. This verse also
tells us to take heart. What does that mean?
I think it means do not despair or don't get discouraged. Again,
that's hard to do!

When I'm waiting for something, like a gift on my birthday, it
takes everything not to open it early! Even worse is if a trip is
coming, it seems like every day is the longest day ever! Is it hard
for you to wait for special or important things?

If we rush things or get impatient, sometimes that special thing
doesn't feel special when it arrives. Or we ruin the surprise and
miss out on all it could have been! Has that ever happened to
you? Let's try hard to wait on the Lord. His timing is always
better than ours because He can see the whole situation, while
we can only see what is right in front of us.

*Lord, help me to wait patiently for what you have planned
for me. Help me to be strong even when I want to rush
ahead. Lord, help me to trust your timing in my life. Amen.*

E**X**alt the Lord our God and worship at his footstool;
He is holy.
Psalms 99:5

To exalt means to 'lift up' someone or something. We are called to lift up God and worship Him. He is holy and worthy of all our praise. Take a moment and think of ways He has helped you, no matter how small you think it is.

If it matters to us, it matters to God.

He loves us unconditionally; nothing can separate us from Him.

Decide today that you will lift Him up every day in every way!

Dear Lord, thank you for who you are and how you have helped me in my life. Thank you for being holy. Please help me to lift you up daily. Amen.

My Thoughts

My Thoughts

_____

_____

_____

_____

_____

_____

_____

_____

_____

_____

_____

_____

_____

_____

Y ou are the light of the world. A city on a hill cannot be hidden. Neither do people light a lamp
and put it under a bowl.
Matthew 5:14

This little light of mine, I'm gonna let it shine!
Let it shine! Let it shine! Let it shine!

That is a song you may have grown up with, learning it at a very young age. Have you thought about what it means? If you accept Christ into your heart, He becomes a light that
should shine through you.

His light should shine through everything you do and say, so people around you will notice that something is different about you. And if they ask about that difference, you can tell them all about your heavenly Father!

If you have been camping or outside at night and used a flashlight, you wouldn't cover it or hide it under a bowl. How would you see where you were going? That also means you should not hide the light of Christ!
You are guiding others to Him!

Father, please help me to shine my light brightly for everyone to see. Help me to live my life so my friends can see something different in me. Show me how to guide them to you, and to spread your light to others. Amen.

It is fine to be Zealous, provided the purpose is good, and to be so always, not just when I am with you.
Galatians 4:18

To be ZEALOUS means to be passionate, enthusiastic or excited about doing something. Christ tells us it is fine to pursue things with passion, as long as those things are good. And He doesn't want us to do good things just when we are seen. We should have the same excitement even when no one is looking.

Maybe you clean your room by pushing things into the closet or under the bed, but if your parents are watching, do you fold your clothes nicely and put things in their rightful place? If you only do the job properly because someone is watching, then you're doing it to be seen and not because it's the right thing to do.

There is nothing wrong with being excited, but make sure you are excited about the right things and for the right reasons.

Lord, help me to do what is right and good with excitement because it is the right thing and not because I want to be seen. Help me to be a reflection of you in all that I do.
Amen.

My Thoughts

My Thoughts

Dear Father,

Thank you for creating me with a special purpose in mind. Thank you for loving me on my good days and on my bad days. Thank you for staying the same and keeping your promises.

I want to live my life in a way that will shine your light for others to see. I want to make you proud. I believe you died and rose again for me. I believe you forgive all my sins and will be waiting for me with open arms one day.

I believe you are who you say you are and I want to give my heart to you today. Please stay with me always, keep me, protect me and guide me.

In Jesus name I pray. Amen.

_____
(Name)

_____
(Date)

Note from the Author

Train up a child in the way that he/she should go, and when they are old they will not depart from it. (Proverbs 22:6)

I am living proof of this verse. I was raised in a Christian home, attended children's church, youth meetings, prayer meetings, EVERY meeting! I had a few years where I did my own thing and then I grew up and remembered the lessons of my youth. By purchasing this book, you are committing to deposit seeds of faith into the life of a child. Maybe that child is yours, maybe this is a gift for another, the bottom line is – you are impacting the direction of the path they will take. Let these verses be a light to that path.

The scriptures chosen are meant to challenge them as they grow, give them a bit more meat than milk!

Hopefully, as you do these lessons, you will have conversations that lead them closer to our Father. As they memorize, so will you. As they learn, so will you. As they grow, so will you! Isn't it funny how that works?

Even if you do not see the results of your labor, remember….

Some plant, some water, but only God can harvest!

Live with impact.

Be Blessed.

Nicole Patrice Thomas

Dear reader,

If you found this book helpful, consider leaving a review so others will be blessed by it as well.

Subscribe to my website and follow me on social media for updates on new releases, events and more!

www.nicolepatricethomas.com
FB, IG, Twitter @nicolepatricet

*WHOLESALE ORDERS AVAILABLE ON REQUEST

Scripture Reference

- Above all else, Guard your heart. For everything you do flows from it. Proverbs:21 NIV

- Be strong and courageous. Don't be afraid, don't be discouraged, for the Lord your God is with you wherever you go. Joshua 1:9 NIV

- Come to me all you who are weary and burdened and I will give you rest.
  Matthew 11:28 NIV

- Do to others what you would have them do to you. Matthew 7:13 NIV

- Everyone who hears these words of mine and puts them into practice is like a wise man who built his house on the rock. Matthew 7:26 NIV

- For I know the plans I have for you, plans to prosper you and not to harm, plans to give you a hope and a future. Jeremiah 29:11 NIV

- Great is our Lord and mighty in power, his understanding has no limit. Psalms 147:5 NIV
- Honor thy father and mother. Exodus 20:12 NIV

- I am the vine, you are the branches. John 15:5 NIV

- Jesus Christ is the same yesterday, and today and forever. Hebrews 13:8 NIV

- Keep your tongue from evil and your lips from telling lies. Psalms 34:13 NIV

- Let your light shine before men, that they may see your good deeds and praise your father in heaven. Matthew 5:16 NIV

- Make a joyful noise unto the Lord. Psalms 98:4 NIV

Scripture Reference

- No man can serve two masters. Matthew 6:24 NIV

- O Give thanks to the Lord, for he is good; His love endures forever. Psalms 118:1 NIV

- Pleasant words are a honeycomb, sweet to the soul and healing to the bones. Proverbs 16:24 NIV
- Quiet words of the wise are more to be heeded than the shouts of a ruler of fools.
  Ecclesiastes 9:17 NIV

- Remember the days of old; consider the generations long past. Ask your father and he will tell you, your elders and they will explain to you. Deuteronomy 32:7 NIV

- Seek first his kingdom and his righteousness, and all these things will be given to you as well. Matthew 6:33 NIV

- The fruit of the spirit is love, joy, peace, patience, kindness, goodness, faithfulness, gentleness and self-control. Galatians 5:22 NIV

- Under his wings you will find refuge. Psalms 91:4 NIV

- Vengeance is mine, says the Lord. Romans 12:9 NIV

- Wait for the Lord; be strong and take heart and wait for the Lord. Psalms 56:3 NIV

- eXalt the Lord our God and worship at his footstool; he is holy. Psalms 99:5 NIV

- You are the light of the world. A city on a hill cannot be hidden. Neither do people light a lamp and put it under a bowl. Matthew 5:14 NIV

- It is fine to be Zealous, provided the purpose is good, and to be so always, not just when I am with you. Galatians 4:18 NIV

OTHER TITLES FROM THIS AUTHOR

CHILDRENS BOOKS

THE FLOWER GIRL COLLECTION - 0-7YRS

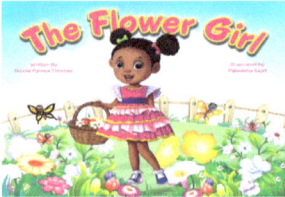

Grace finds herself in trouble when she does not follow the rules her mother gave her. As she tries to fix her problems on her own, things get even worse! With the help of kind animals she meets along the way, Grace's obedience will once again be tested. Will she be able to get out of trouble? Will she learn to obey?

*Picturebook Available in English and Spanish

It's your turn! Lets get creative and learn as you color!

This companion to the picture book, The Flower Girl, is sure to delight and entertain your young reader while providing fun moments to learn art, science, writing, math and reading skills. There are pages to help children think about gratefulness and define their likes or dislikes. This activity book will also provide opportunities for adults to teach children their address, who to ask for help and how to contact you in the event of an emergency.

A book that will have far reaching benefits when added to your bookshelf!

OTHER TITLES FROM THIS AUTHOR

YOUNG ADULT CHRISTIAN FANTASY

TALES OF ELHAANAI SERIES - 16+

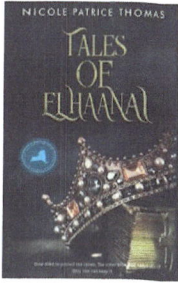

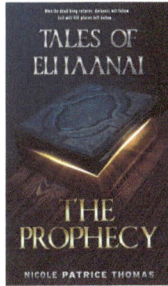

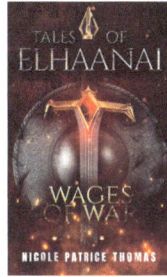

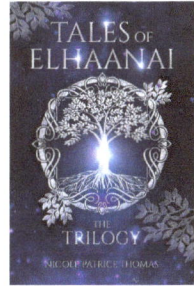

Readers will be swept away to the magical realm of Elhaanai, where tales of love, betrayal, and the struggle for power unfold in this epic three-part saga. Follow three mothers who push the boundaries of maternal love, while their sons struggle against light and darkness. With each chapter you will discover that these characters are not the villains or heroes we expect them to be.

With all three books in one stunning hardcover volume, Tales of Elhaanai offers a deep dive into the intricate histories and mythologies of this fantastical world. This series immerses readers in a rich tapestry of faith, magic and intrigue.

For fans of fantasy series like Game of Thrones, Harry Potter and The Lord of the Rings, Tales of Elhaanai is a must-read. Prepare to be swept up in a world of political machinations, self discovery and a battle for the soul of a nation that will keeping you reading until the final page.

www.ingramcontent.com/pod-product-compliance
Lightning Source LLC
Chambersburg PA
CBHW041917260326
41914CB00014B/1485